This Planner belongs to

_____
_____

Copyright 2019 by Self Reflection Books.
All Rights Reserved.
Cover Image by vecteezy.com

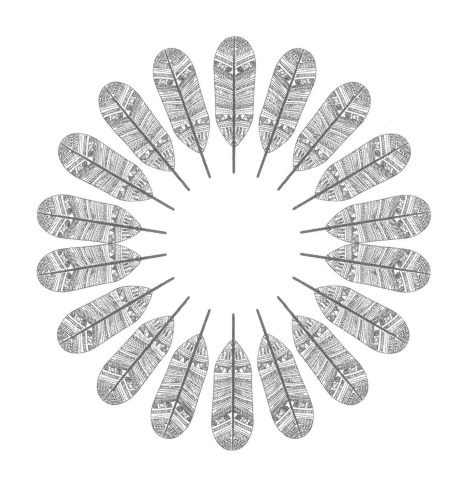

"Yoga is like music.
The rhythm of the body, the melody of the mind and the harmony of the soul, create the symphony of life."

BKS Iyengar

Table of content

PAGE

Table of content

PAGE

Table of content

PAGE

Table of content

PAGE

CLASS PLAN

Date/Time: 11-3 @ 9:30
Venue: MHC

Level:
Duration: 45
Attendees: 3
Private Class: Y/(N)

Class Theme: Autumn
Letting go of old or what doesn't serve us preparing for the new

Mantra / Positive Quote:

Music:

Oils: lavender

Props: Blocks, bolster, knee cushion

Sequence:

> "Do not speak unless it improves on silence."
> — Buddhist proverb

Notes
Opening ② Seated side stretches
③ Cat/cow to childs
① Shoulder roles & release
Table top - spinal balance
Gate pose
Low lunge
½ seated splits
Sun A to Mountain, step back to Downdog - W1   R/L x 2
W2
Extended side

② Malasana 2 min
① Tree x 1 min R/L (ankle rolls)
Wide FF seated
Tree (seated)
Butterfly (FF opt)
Reclining or side lying savasana

CLASS PLAN

Level: pre
Duration: 45

Date/Time: 11/17/2022
Venue: ....

Attendees: ....
Private Class: Y/N

Class Theme:
Shoulder and back tension
Focus on breath, surrender & acceptance

Mantra / Positive Quote:

Music:

Oils:

Props:
Block, bolster, knee pad

Sequence:

Shoulder rolls 5 each way
Shoulders to ears 5
Seated cat & cow 5
Hands behind hips, knees bent, rotate wrist w/ gentle pressure 10 breathes each
Puppy pose · opt to be on forearms
extend arms, then interlock finger, bend elbows
bring hands behind head 20 breaths

> "Success is the sum of small efforts,
> Repeated day-in and day-out."
> — Robert Collier

Notes

- TT, rock back on heels
- Malasana to ½ lift (Hold Malasana 20 breath)
- Use blocks on ½ lift or hands on thigh
- Rise, arms over head, interlace
- Take side bend R/L
- Standing Sun ▲ - FF, ½ lift, rise
- 3 to 5 times
- Goddess 10 breaths, rise - use block to walk forward to wide FF, slight traction in back
- Repeat Goddess x 2 - add 10 breathes each time
- Repeat wide FF after 20 & 30 ↑
- Goddess - hands on knees,
    - L/shoulder toward R knee, 10 breathes
    - R/shoulder toward L knee, 10 breathes
- Repeat 2·3 x's
- TT - figure 8 hips R/L 2x's each side
- Seated twist R elbow to R knee
    - L hand behind L hip, gaze over L
- Reverse TT
- Wide FF, use block for head or lean back
- ½ pigeon w/ bolster under front leg
- Seated Square
- Recline legs up wall", bottom slightly away
- Roll to Left Side

CLASS PLAN

Level: ....
Duration: ....

Date/Time: ....
Venue: ....

Attendees: ....
Private Class: Y/N

Class Theme:

Mantra / Positive Quote:

Music:

Oils:

Props:
....
....
....

Sequence:

"Choose to be optimistic, it feels better."

— Dalai Lama

Notes

Warm up - Shoulder & wrist roles
  spinal balance to compass pose
  gate pose

Sun A - use block in FF if needed
side body stretch

Sun B - low lunge
  rise to Crescent (interlace & side stretch)
    Straighten to lunge x 3
  modified W3
    W2 (straighten x 3)
  Extended side angle
  Triangle
  W2
  FF wide side, shift side to side
Move freely, organic,
  * Chair (hold) arms sweep

Malasana
Seated Butterfly
tree pose - FF toward straight leg
bridge
Happy baby

CLASS PLAN

Level: ....
Duration: ....

Date/Time: ....
Venue: ....

Attendees: ....
Private Class: Y/N

Class Theme:

Mantra / Positive Quote:

Music:

Oils:

Props:
....
....
....

Sequence:

"Yoga is the perfect opportunity to be curious about who you are."

Jason Crandell

Notes

CLASS PLAN

Level:
Duration:

Date/Time: ....
Venue: ....

Attendees: ....
Private Class: Y/N

Class Theme:

Mantra / Positive Quote:

Music:

Oils:

Props:
....
....
....

Sequence:

Notes

"Yoga is the journey of the self,
through the self, to the self."
The Bhagavad Gita

CLASS PLAN

Level:
Duration:

Date/Time: ....
Venue: ....

Attendees: ....
Private Class: Y/N

Class Theme:

Mantra / Positive Quote:

Music:

Oils:

Props:
....
....
....

Sequence:

"The quieter you become the more you are able to hear."

Notes

Rumi

CLASS PLAN

Level
Duration

Date/Time: ....
Venue: ....

Attendees: ....
Private Class: Y/N

Class Theme:

Mantra / Positive Quote:

Music:

Oils:

Props:
....
....
....

Sequence:

"The attitude of gratitude is the highest yoga."
— Yogi Bhajan

Notes

CLASS PLAN

Level ......
Duration ......

Date/Time: ....
Venue: ....

Attendees: ....
Private Class: Y/N

Class Theme:

Mantra / Positive Quote:

Music:

Oils:

Props:
....
....
....

Sequence:

"The gift of learning to meditate is the greatest gift you can give yourself in this lifetime."
Sogyal Rinpoche

Notes

CLASS PLAN

Level: ....
Duration: ....

Date/Time: ....
Venue: ....
Attendees: ....
Private Class: Y/N

Class Theme:

Mantra / Positive Quote:

Music:

Oils:

Props:
....
....
....

Sequence:

"Yoga teaches us to cure what need not be endured and endure what cannot be cured."

Notes   BKS Iyengar

CLASS PLAN

Level:
Duration:

Date/Time: ....
Venue: ....

Attendees: ....
Private Class: Y/N

Class Theme:

Mantra / Positive Quote:

Music:

Oils:

Props:
....
....
....

Sequence:

"Yoga is the fountain of youth. You're only as young as your spine is flexible."

Bob Harper

Notes

CLASS PLAN

Level ......
Duration ......

Date/Time: ....
Venue: ....

Attendees: ....
Private Class: Y/N

Class Theme:

Mantra / Positive Quote:

Music:

Oils:

Props:
....
....
....

Sequence:

"The way to love anything is to realize that it might be lost."
G.K. Chesterton

Notes

CLASS PLAN

Level ....
Duration ....

Date/Time: ....
Venue: ....

Attendees: ....
Private Class: Y/N

Class Theme:

Mantra / Positive Quote:

Music:

Oils:

Props:
....
....
....

Sequence:

"Blessed is the influence of one true, loving human soul to another."

George Elliot

Notes

CLASS PLAN

Date/Time: ....
Venue: ....

Level ▭
Duration ▭

Attendees: ....
Private Class: Y/N

Class Theme:

Mantra / Positive Quote:

Music:

Oils:

Props:
....
....
....

Sequence:

"Creating space frees the spirit to bring in what it truly desires."

Notes

Deb Reble

CLASS PLAN

Level: ……
Duration: ……

Date/Time: ……………………
Venue: ……………………

Attendees: ……………
Private Class: Y/N

Class Theme:

Mantra / Positive Quote:

Music:

Oils:

Props:
....
....
....

Sequence:

"Yoga is almost like music in a way; there's no end to it."

Notes

Sting

CLASS PLAN

Level: ....
Duration: ....

Date/Time: ....
Venue: ....

Attendees: ....
Private Class: Y/N

Class Theme:

Mantra / Positive Quote:

Music:

Oils:

Props:
....
....
....

Sequence:

"Even if things don't unfold the way you expected, don't be disheartened or give up. One who continues to advance will win in the end."
— Daisaku Ikeda

Notes

CLASS PLAN

Level ....
Duration ....

Date/Time: ....
Venue: ....

Attendees: ....
Private Class: Y/N

Class Theme:

Mantra / Positive Quote:

Music:

Oils:

Props:
....
....
....

Sequence:

"Life is meant to be lived. Curiosity must be kept alive. One must never, for whatever reason, turn his back on life." — Eleanor Roosevelt

Notes

CLASS PLAN

Date/Time: ....
Venue: ....

Level:
Duration:
Attendees: ....
Private Class: Y/N

Class Theme:

Mantra / Positive Quote:

Music:

Oils:

Props:
....
....
....

Sequence:

"Nothing ever is, but is always becoming."
Plato

Notes

CLASS PLAN

Level ....
Duration ....

Date/Time: ....
Venue: ....

Attendees: ....
Private Class: Y/N

Class Theme:

Mantra / Positive Quote:

Music:

Oils:

Props:

....
....
....

Sequence:

"You only lose what you cling to."
Siddhārtha Gautama Buddha

Notes

CLASS PLAN

Level: ....
Duration: ....

Date/Time: ....
Venue: ....

Attendees: ....
Private Class: Y/N

Class Theme:

Mantra / Positive Quote:

Music:

Oils:

Props:
....
....
....

Sequence:

"She was unstoppable, not because she did not have failures and doubts, but because she continued on despite of them."

Beau Taplin

Notes

CLASS PLAN

Level: ....
Duration: ....

Date/Time: ....
Venue: ....

Attendees: ....
Private Class: Y/N

Class Theme:

Mantra / Positive Quote:

Music:

Oils:

Props:
....
....
....

Sequence:

"We are not going in circles, we are going upwards. The path is a spiral; we have already climbed many steps."
— Hermann Hesse

Notes

CLASS PLAN

Level: ......
Duration: ......

Date/Time: ....
Venue: ....

Attendees: ....
Private Class: Y/N

Class Theme:

Mantra / Positive Quote:

Music:

Oils:

Props:
....
....
....

Sequence:

"Don't move the way fear makes you move. Move the way love makes you move. Move the way joy makes you move."

Notes

Osho

CLASS PLAN

Level
Duration

Date/Time: ....
Venue: ....

Attendees: ....
Private Class: Y/N

Class Theme:

Mantra / Positive Quote:

Music:

Oils:

Props:
....
....
....

Sequence:

Notes

"Peace comes from within.
Do not seek it without."
Gautama Buddha

CLASS PLAN

Level
Duration

Date/Time: ....
Venue: ....

Attendees: ....
Private Class: Y/N

Class Theme:

Mantra / Positive Quote:

Music:

Oils:

Props:
....
....
....

Sequence:

"The successful warrior is the average man, with laser-like focus."

Bruce Lee

Notes

CLASS PLAN

Level ......
Duration ......

Date/Time: ....
Venue: ....

Attendees: ....
Private Class: Y/N

Class Theme:

Mantra / Positive Quote:

Music:

Oils:

Props:
....
....
....

Sequence:

> "Silence is not silent. Silence speaks. It speaks most eloquently. Silence is not still. Silence leads. It leads most perfectly."
>
> — Sri Chinmoy

Notes

CLASS PLAN

Level: ....
Duration: ....

Date/Time: ....
Venue: ....

Attendees: ....
Private Class: Y/N

Class Theme:

Mantra / Positive Quote:

Music:

Oils:

Props:

....
....
....

Sequence:

> "Fear less, hope more; eat less, chew more; whine less, breathe more; talk less, say more; hate less, love more; and all good things are yours."
> — Swedish Proverb

Notes

CLASS PLAN

Level: ......
Duration: ......

Date/Time: ....
Venue: ....

Attendees: ....
Private Class: Y/N

Class Theme:

Mantra / Positive Quote:

Music:

Oils:

Props:
....
....
....

Sequence:

> "Motivation is what gets you started.
> Habit is what keeps you going."
>
> — Jim Ryun

Notes

CLASS PLAN

Level: ....
Duration: ....

Date/Time: ....
Venue: ....

Attendees: ....
Private Class: Y/N

Class Theme:

Mantra / Positive Quote:

Music:

Oils:

Props:
....
....
....

Sequence:

"Happiness is not a state to arrive at, but a manner of traveling."

Margaret Lee Runbeck

Notes

CLASS PLAN

Level: ....
Duration: ....

Date/Time: ....
Venue: ....

Attendees: ....
Private Class: Y/N

Class Theme:

Mantra / Positive Quote:

Music:

Oils:

Props:
....
....
....

Sequence:

"Do not feel lonely,
the entire universe is inside you."
Rumi

Notes

Class Plan

Level:
Duration:

Date/Time: ....
Venue: ....

Attendees: ....
Private Class: Y/N

Class Theme:

Mantra / Positive Quote:

Music:

Oils:

Props:

....
....
....

Sequence:

"Suffering usually relates to wanting things to be different from the way they are."

— Allan Lokos

Notes

CLASS PLAN

Level: ....
Duration: ....

Date/Time: ....
Venue: ....

Attendees: ....
Private Class: Y/N

Class Theme:

Mantra / Positive Quote:

Music:

Oils:

Props:
....
....
....

Sequence:

"Meditation is to be aware of every thought and of every feeling, never to say it is right or wrong, but just to watch it and to move with it." — Krishnamurti

Notes

CLASS PLAN

Level:
Duration:

Date/Time: ....
Venue: ....

Attendees: ....
Private Class: Y/N

Class Theme:

Mantra / Positive Quote:

Music:

Oils:

Props:

....
....
....

Sequence:

"In the midst of movement and chaos,
keep stillness inside of you."

Deepak Chopra

Notes

CLASS PLAN

Level: ......
Duration: ......

Date/Time: ....
Venue: ....

Attendees: ....
Private Class: Y/N

Class Theme:

Mantra / Positive Quote:

Music:

Oils:

Props:
....
....
....

Sequence:

"Happiness is an inside job."

William Arthur Ward

Notes

CLASS PLAN

Level ....
Duration ....

Date/Time: ....
Venue: ....

Attendees: ....
Private Class: Y/N

Class Theme:

Mantra / Positive Quote:

Music:

Oils:

Props:
....
....
....

Sequence:

"Make the driving force in your life love."
— Dr. Oz

Notes

CLASS PLAN

Level: ....
Duration: ....

Date/Time: ....
Venue: ....

Attendees: ....
Private Class: Y/N

Class Theme:

Mantra / Positive Quote:

Music:

Oils:

Props:
....
....
....

Sequence:

"Intelligence comes into being when the mind, the heart and the body are really harmonious."

Krishnamurti

Notes

Class Plan

Level: ....
Duration: ....

Date/Time: ....
Venue: ....

Attendees: ....
Private Class: Y/N

Class Theme:

Mantra / Positive Quote:

Music:

Oils:

Props:
....
....
....

Sequence:

"All progress takes place outside the comfort zone."
Michael John Bobak

Notes

CLASS PLAN

Level:
Duration:

Date/Time: ....
Venue: ....

Attendees: ....
Private Class: Y/N

Class Theme:

Mantra / Positive Quote:

Music:

Oils:

Props:
....
....
....

Sequence:

"Take the time to just do nothing. It will open up a completely new world of insight for you."

Scott Shaw

Notes

CLASS PLAN

Level: ....
Duration: ....

Date/Time: ....
Venue: ....

Attendees: ....
Private Class: Y/N

Class Theme:

Mantra / Positive Quote:

Music:

Oils:

Props:
....
....
....

Sequence:

"The yoga pose that you avoid the most you need the most."

Anonymous

Notes

CLASS PLAN

Level ......
Duration ......

Date/Time: ....
Venue: ....

Attendees: ....
Private Class: Y/N

Class Theme:

Mantra / Positive Quote:

Music:

Oils:

Props:
....
....
....

Sequence:

> "Take care of your body. It's the only place you have to live."
> — Jim Rohn

Notes

CLASS PLAN

Level: ......
Duration: ......

Date/Time: ....
Venue: ....

Attendees: ....
Private Class: Y/N

Class Theme:

Mantra / Positive Quote:

Music:

Oils:

Props:
....
....
....

Sequence:

"Each morning we are born again. What we do today is what matters most."

— Buddha

Notes

Class Plan

Level:
Duration:

Date/Time: ....
Venue: ....

Attendees: ....
Private Class: Y/N

Class Theme:

Mantra / Positive Quote:

Music:

Oils:

Props:
....
....
....

Sequence:

"Happiness is a state of inner fulfillment, not the gratification of inexhaustible desires for outward things."

Matthieu Ricard

Notes

CLASS PLAN

Level
Duration

Date/Time: ....
Venue: ....

Attendees: ....
Private Class: Y/N

Class Theme:

Mantra / Positive Quote:

Music:

Oils:

Props:
....
....
....

Sequence:

"Through meditation and by giving full attention to one thing at a time, we can learn to direct attention where we choose." — Eknath Easwaran

Notes

CLASS PLAN

Level
Duration

Date/Time: ....
Venue: ....

Attendees: ....
Private Class: Y/N

Class Theme:

Mantra / Positive Quote:

Music:

Oils:

Props:
....
....
....

Sequence:

"You can do anything, but not everything."

Anonymous

Notes

CLASS PLAN

Level
Duration

Date/Time: ....
Venue: ....

Attendees: ....
Private Class: Y/N

Class Theme:

Mantra / Positive Quote:

Music:

Oils:

Props:
....
....
....

Sequence:

"What seems to us as bitter trials are often blessings in disguise."

Oscar Wilde

Notes

CLASS PLAN

Level
Duration

Date/Time: ....
Venue: ....

Attendees: ....
Private Class: Y/N

Class Theme:

Mantra / Positive Quote:

Music:

Oils:

Props:
....
....
....

Sequence:

"Whenever you see a successful person you only see the public glories, never the private sacrifices to reach them."
— Vaibhav Shah

Notes

CLASS PLAN

Level:
Duration:

Date/Time: ....
Venue: ....

Attendees: ....
Private Class: Y/N

Class Theme:

Mantra / Positive Quote:

Music:

Oils:

Props:
....
....
....

Sequence:

"Don't waste a good mistake. Learn from it."

Robert Kiyosaki

Notes

CLASS PLAN

Level ....
Duration ....

Date/Time: ....
Venue: ....

Attendees: ....
Private Class: Y/N

Class Theme:

Mantra / Positive Quote:

Music:

Oils:

Props:
....
....
....

Sequence:

"The present moment is filled with joy and happiness. If you are attentive, you will see it."

Thich Nhat Hanh

Notes

CLASS PLAN

Level ....
Duration ....

Date/Time: ....
Venue: ....

Attendees: ....
Private Class: Y/N

Class Theme:

Mantra / Positive Quote:

Music:

Oils:

Props:

....
....
....

Sequence:

"The beauty is that people often come here for the stretch, and leave with a lot more"

Liza Ciano

Notes

CLASS PLAN

Level: ....
Duration: ....

Date/Time: ....
Venue: ....

Attendees: ....
Private Class: Y/N

Class Theme:

Mantra / Positive Quote:

Music:

Oils:

Props:
....
....
....

Sequence:

"Yoga is invigoration in relaxation. Freedom in routine. Confidence through self control. Energy within and energy without." — Ymber Delecto

Notes

CLASS PLAN

Level: ....
Duration: ....

Date/Time: ....
Venue: ....

Attendees: ....
Private Class: Y/N

Class Theme:

Mantra / Positive Quote:

Music:

Oils:

Props:
....
....
....

Sequence:

"Don't just do something—sit there!"

UNKNOWN Yoga Quote

Notes

CLASS PLAN

Level
Duration

Date/Time: ....
Venue: ....

Attendees: ....
Private Class: Y/N

Class Theme:

Mantra / Positive Quote:

Music:

Oils:

Props:
....
....
....

Sequence:

"The meaning of life is to find your gift.
The purpose of life is to give it away."
Anonymous

Notes

CLASS PLAN

Level:
Duration:

Date/Time: ....
Venue: ....

Attendees: ....
Private Class: Y/N

Class Theme:

Mantra / Positive Quote:

Music:

Oils:

Props:
....
....
....

Sequence:

"Meditation stills the wandering mind and establishes us forever in a state of peace."
— Muktananda

Notes

CLASS PLAN

Level:
Duration:

Date/Time: ....
Venue: ....

Attendees: ....
Private Class: Y/N

Class Theme:

Mantra / Positive Quote:

Music:

Oils:

Props:

....
....
....

Sequence:

"The most important pieces of equipment you need for doing yoga are your body and your mind."

Notes

Rodney Yee

CLASS PLAN

Level ....
Duration ....

Date/Time: ....
Venue: ....

Attendees: ....
Private Class: Y/N

Class Theme:

Mantra / Positive Quote:

Music:

Oils:

Props:
....
....
....

Sequence:

"We don't realize that, somewhere within us all, there does exist a supreme self who is eternally at peace."

Notes

Eat, Pray, Love

CLASS PLAN

Level ......
Duration ......

Date/Time: ....
Venue: ....

Attendees: ....
Private Class: Y/N

Class Theme:

Mantra / Positive Quote:

Music:

Oils:

Props:
....
....
....

Sequence:

"If you change the way you look at things, the things you look at change."

Wayne Dyer

Notes

CLASS PLAN

Level: ....
Duration: ....

Date/Time: ....
Venue: ....

Attendees: ....
Private Class: Y/N

Class Theme:

Mantra / Positive Quote:

Music:

Oils:

Props:
....
....
....

Sequence:

"You can't lead anyone else further than you have gone yourself."
— Gene Mauch

Notes

CLASS PLAN

Level ......
Duration ......

Date/Time: ....
Venue: ....

Attendees: ....
Private Class: Y/N

Class Theme:

Mantra / Positive Quote:

Music:

Oils:

Props:
....
....
....

Sequence:

"He who has health has hope and he who has hope has everything."
Arabian Proverb

Notes

CLASS PLAN

Level:
Duration:

Date/Time: ....
Venue: ....

Attendees: ....
Private Class: Y/N

Class Theme:

Mantra / Positive Quote:

Music:

Oils:

Props:
....
....
....

Sequence:

"Our bodies are our gardens—our wills are our gardeners."
Shakespeare

Notes

CLASS PLAN

Date/Time: ....
Venue: ....

Level:
Duration:
Attendees: ....
Private Class: Y/N

Class Theme:

Mantra / Positive Quote:

Music:

Oils:

Props:
....
....
....

Sequence:

"The future belongs to those who believe in the beauty of their dreams"

Eleanor Roosevelt

Notes

CLASS PLAN

Level: ......
Duration: ......

Date/Time: ....
Venue: ....

Attendees: ....
Private Class: Y/N

Class Theme:

Mantra / Positive Quote:

Music:

Oils:

Props:
....
....
....

Sequence:

"The part can never be well unless the whole is well."

Plato

Notes

CLASS PLAN

Level ......
Duration ......

Date/Time: ....
Venue: ....

Attendees: ....
Private Class: Y/N

Class Theme:

Mantra / Positive Quote:

Music:

Oils:

Props:

....
....
....

Sequence:

"We tend to think of meditation in only one way. But life itself is a meditation."

— Raul Julia

Notes

CLASS PLAN

Level:
Duration:

Date/Time: ....
Venue: ....

Attendees: ....
Private Class: Y/N

Class Theme:

Mantra / Positive Quote:

Music:

Oils:

Props:
....
....
....

Sequence:

"Meditation is painful in the beginning but it bestows immortal bliss and supreme joy in the end."

Swami Sivananda

Notes

CLASS PLAN

Level: ....
Duration: ....

Date/Time: ....
Venue: ....

Attendees: ....
Private Class: Y/N

Class Theme:

Mantra / Positive Quote:

Music:

Oils:

Props:
....
....
....

Sequence:

"Nowhere can man find a quieter or more untroubled retreat than in his own soul."
— Marcus Aurelius

Notes

CLASS PLAN

Level ....
Duration ....

Date/Time: ....
Venue: ....

Attendees: ....
Private Class: Y/N

Class Theme:

Mantra / Positive Quote:

Music:

Oils:

Props:
....
....
....

Sequence:

"Travel light, live light, spread the light, be the light."

Yogi Bhajan

Notes

CLASS PLAN

Level: ....
Duration: ....

Date/Time: ....
Venue: ....

Attendees: ....
Private Class: Y/N

Class Theme:

Mantra / Positive Quote:

Music:

Oils:

Props:
....
....
....

Sequence:

> "When breath control is correct, mind control is possible."
>
> — Pattabhi Jois

Notes

CLASS PLAN

Level: ....
Duration: ....

Date/Time: ....
Venue: ....

Attendees: ....
Private Class: Y/N

Class Theme:

Mantra / Positive Quote:

Music:

Oils:

Props:
....
....
....

Sequence:

"Yoga is not about self-improvement, it's about self-acceptance."

Gurmukh Kaur Khalsa

Notes

CLASS PLAN

Level:
Duration:

Date/Time: ....
Venue: ....

Attendees: ....
Private Class: Y/N

Class Theme:

Mantra / Positive Quote:

Music:

Oils:

Props:
....
....
....

Sequence:

"Life is a school of probability."

Walter Bagehot

Notes

CLASS PLAN

Level ....
Duration ....

Date/Time: ....
Venue: ....

Attendees: ....
Private Class: Y/N

Class Theme:

Mantra / Positive Quote:

Music:

Oils:

Props:
....
....
....

Sequence:

"Meditation is such a more substantial reality than what we normally take to be reality."
— Richard Gere

Notes

CLASS PLAN

Level ....
Duration ....

Date/Time: ....
Venue: ....

Attendees: ....
Private Class: Y/N

Class Theme:

Mantra / Positive Quote:

Music:

Oils:

Props:
....
....
....

Sequence:

"The affairs of the world will go on forever.
Do not delay the practice of meditation."
— Milarepa

Notes

CLASS PLAN

Level:
Duration:

Date/Time: ....
Venue: ....

Attendees: ....
Private Class: Y/N

Class Theme:

Mantra / Positive Quote:

Music:

Oils:

Props:
....
....
....

Sequence:

"Yoga began with the first person wanting to be healthy and happy all the time."
Sri Swami Satchidananda

Notes

CLASS PLAN

Level: ......
Duration: ......

Date/Time: ....
Venue: ....

Attendees: ....
Private Class: Y/N

Class Theme:

Mantra / Positive Quote:

Music:

Oils:

Props:
....
....
....

Sequence:

"There are different things one can do to establish and hasten the peace process. Meditation is one way."

— Mike Love

Notes

CLASS PLAN

Level ......
Duration ......

Date/Time: ....
Venue: ....

Attendees: ....
Private Class: Y/N

Class Theme:

Mantra / Positive Quote:

Music:

Oils:

Props:
....
....
....

Sequence:

"The yoga mat is a good place to turn when talk therapy and antidepressants aren't enough."

— Amy Weintraub

Notes

CLASS PLAN

Level ......
Duration ......

Date/Time: ....
Venue: ....

Attendees: ....
Private Class: Y/N

Class Theme:

Mantra / Positive Quote:

Music:

Oils:

Props:
....
....
....

Sequence:

"Reading makes a full man, meditation a profound man, discourse a clear man."

Benjamin Franklin

Notes

CLASS PLAN

Level: ....
Duration: ....

Date/Time: ....
Venue: ....

Attendees: ....
Private Class: Y/N

Class Theme:

Mantra / Positive Quote:

Music:

Oils:

Props:
....
....
....

Sequence:

"The very heart of yoga practice is 'abyhasa' steady effort in the direction you want to go."
— Sally Kempton

Notes

CLASS PLAN

Date/Time: ....

Venue: ....

Level:
Duration:
Attendees: ....
Private Class: Y/N

Class Theme:

Mantra / Positive Quote:

Music:

Oils:

Props:

....
....
....

Sequence:

"Yoga means addition. Addition of energy, strength and beauty to body, mind and soul."

Amit Ray

Notes

CLASS PLAN

Level: ......
Duration: ......

Date/Time: ....
Venue: ....

Attendees: ....
Private Class: Y/N

Class Theme:

Mantra / Positive Quote:

Music:

Oils:

Props:

....
....
....

Sequence:

> "Calming the mind is yoga. Not just standing on the head."
>
> Swami Satchidananda

Notes

CLASS PLAN

Level: ......
Duration: ......

Date/Time: ....
Venue: ....

Attendees: ....
Private Class: Y/N

Class Theme:

Mantra / Positive Quote:

Music:

Oils:

Props:
....
....
....

Sequence:

"In truth yoga doesn't take time
— it gives time."
Ganga White

Notes

CLASS PLAN

Level .....
Duration .....

Date/Time: ....
Venue: ....

Attendees: ....
Private Class: Y/N

Class Theme:

Mantra / Positive Quote:

Music:

Oils:

Props:

....
....
....

Sequence:

"Yoga does not just change the way we see things, it transforms the person who sees."

BKS Iyengar

Notes

CLASS PLAN

Level:
Duration:

Date/Time: ....
Venue: ....

Attendees: ....
Private Class: Y/N

Class Theme:

Mantra / Positive Quote:

Music:

Oils:

Props:
....
....
....

Sequence:

"Meditation brings wisdom; lack of meditation leaves ignorance."

— Buddha

Notes

Made in the USA
Coppell, TX
27 May 2022